IN SICKNESS
AND IN HEALTH

IN SICKNESS
AND IN HEALTH

How to Cope When
Your Loved One Is Ill

 Earl A. Grollman

BEACON PRESS   BOSTON

Beacon Press
25 Beacon Street
Boston, Massachusetts 02108

Beacon Press books are published under the auspices
of the Unitarian Universalist Association
of Congregations in North America.

94 93 92 91 90 89 88 87   8 7 6 5 4 3 2 1

Library of Congress Cataloging-in-Publication Data

Grollman, Earl A.
    In sickness and in health.

    Rev. ed. of: When your loved one is dying. © 1980.
    1. Death—Social aspects—United States. 2. Death—
United States—Psychological aspects. 3. Terminally ill—
United States—Family relationships. I. Grollman,
Earl A. When your loved one is dying. II. Title.
HQ1073.5.U6G76   1987   155.9'37   87-1136
ISBN 0-8070-2705-7 (pbk.)

In memory of Saul Lipton

Contents

What this book is about . . .

Someone in your family or a close friend is suffering from serious illness. This has an upsetting and disruptive effect not only on the sick person, but on the family and friends as well.

You may say: "I never imagined it could be like this."

The purpose of this book is to assist you in moving from helplessness to helpfulness; to help you cope with your own emotional upheaval; and better understand the needs of your loved one.

IMPACT
AND GRIEF

Your Needs When Your Loved One Is Seriously Ill

If you want life,
expect pain.

—MARTIN BUBER

Your loved one is very sick.

You feel as though you have fallen
into a dark pit,
separated from everyone and everything.

My God, my God,
Why hast Thou forsaken me?
I cry by day,
but Thou dost not answer,
and by night,
but find no rest.
                    —*Psalm 22*

Time stands still.
The real seems so unreal.

You want to cry out
But your throat is tight.

Your lips move.
But no sound comes forth.

Your body is frozen.

A huge stone has settled in
your stomach.

Gradually,
emotions rush over you,
invading and holding you
in the grip of
anger and anguish,
fear and frustration,
dread and despair.

You are afraid
you will lose control,
be swept away by
overpowering emotions.

You keep repeating:

"My loved one is sick.
My loved one is sick.
My loved one is sick,"

as if the sounds
of these frightening words
will enable you to
understand and accept
the terrifying truth.

But speech brings
little comfort or consolation.

You are in
excruciating pain.

The sting of serious illness
is real.

You fear
that your loved one
may never recover.

Loss of health
squeezes the life out of you.

The more your life is bound up
with your beloved
the more vulnerable you are
to grief.

You can't imagine the fact that your beloved
will not be able to share
your life together
in the way you once knew.

You want your lives
to be as before

dreams came crashing down.

"I wish I were sick instead."

Why pretend that you are not experiencing
difficult feelings
during painful moments?

Is it because you feel
so vulnerable?

Is it because
you are afraid of the reactions of others?

Have you been taught
that being strong
means *not* to show feeling?

It is *normal* to grieve.

When a loved one is in poor health,
it's like losing a part of your self.

You have
a deep personal investment in your relationship.

You don't want to lose it.

Grief is an adaptive
response to loss.

Social scientists call it
"anticipatory" or "preparatory grief"—
the working through of your sorrow
as a rehearsal for a doubtful future.

Your anticipation and preparation
help you to
understand and cope
with the impact of your possible loss.

You have every right
to feel the weight of depression.

You grieve
because
you love.

You feel like a victim
of a sudden windstorm—
swept away by forces
you didn't expect and
can't control.

Not everyone will understand
your needs.

Some people may say to you,
"Don't be depressed,"
or
"Don't act so angry."

Some people will
feel uncomfortable
with your frustration and unhappiness.

But rest assured:
your grief is a normal process
of waves and sensations
that spin you around
in an emotional whirlpool.

How you confront your feelings
depends upon so many factors:

the way you normally handle stress,
the severity of your loved one's illness, and
the support of your friends, medical staff,
and family.

Even though grief is
a common human experience,
it is as individual
as fingerprints—
appearing in
widely varying combinations.

As you experience
some of the emotions associated
with grief,
you may feel like a cork bobbing erratically
on a sea of conflicting emotions.

Unreality

You hear the diagnosis of the illness
but don't feel it.

You cry in a detached way
devoid of any sense
of what is happening
to your loved one
and to you.

You feel numb.

An initial phase of grief
is a sense of unreality,
serving as a built-in buffer
to help you weather the storm.

Numbness affords a respite—
an emotional suspension—
before you go forward
to accept the crushing news
of your loved one's sickness.

Disbelief

If you accept reality,
you might have to exchange
your numbness for pain.

It's hard to accept things
you don't want to be true.

"I *can't* believe it."
"I *won't* believe it."
"I *don't* believe it."

"There might be some mistake.
The medical reports are mixed up
with someone else's.

We'll get a second opinion
—or a third—

There *must* be something
they can do."

You dream at night,
that your loved one is healthy,
just fine.

You take every small improvement
as a sign that your loved one
is now better.
"God wouldn't let this
happen to me *now!*"

Just as you may close your eyes
when something offends your sight,
so are you now refusing to accept

what your mind knows to be true.

Denial isn't
an all-or-nothing affair.

You may have moments of acceptance
when you think about the severity of the illness.

Alternately,
there could be disbelief
as you plan for
the far-off future—*together*,
just as before.

"This is a nightmare.
Please let me wake up
and find things just as they were before."

Fantasies make acceptance
a slow process.

But eventually you will be able to say,
"My loved one is very sick."

This admission is a
landmark
in your journey.

Panic

Acceptance, though, doesn't always
bring peace.
"Why can't I get hold of myself?"

Your physical and emotional
resources are stretched to the limit.

You feel like
you are losing control.

You feel helpless and disorganized.

"If only I could run away,
anywhere."

You need time to
collect yourself.

Hostility

When
    a mother's beauty fades,
    a strong father becomes frail,
    a child's hair falls out,

your sense of helplessness may turn to rage.

"Why me?
 Why my beloved?
 What did *we* do to deserve this?"

You may be infuriated with
the doctors and nurses,
   for not doing more,
the clergy,
   whose intervention has failed,
God,
   for being unjust,
friends and neighbors,
   who seem healthy and happy.

You may even be angry with your loved one,
for becoming gravely ill
and spoiling future plans.

And you are furious with yourself
for feeling furious.

Your nerves are constantly on edge.
Little things disturb you.

Anger comes unexpectedly and
is hard to contain.
You feel a lingering bitterness.

"I don't deserve this."

Rage
helps you to release
your anguish and frustration
at your inability
to *do* something about it.

Holding back your anger too much
can lead to a deep depression.

Depression

Your emotions are beaten down.
You have the sickening feeling
of going down, down, down.

Silence in solitude
is preferable to the burden of
socializing with friends.

You feel overwhelmed—drained.

Nothing matters anymore.
Nothing.

"Life will *never* be worth living."

Depression colors
everything you do and think.

Hopelessness
hangs around your neck
like an albatross.

Every cloud does *not* have a silver lining.
When there is inner and outer turmoil,
no cloud has a silver lining.

Depression is anger turned inward,
a kind of frozen rage.

It is not only a normal response to anticipated
loss,
but a psychological necessity
for working through your pain.

Now you are facing reality.
You are suffering.
The truth *has* registered.
The signs are impossible to ignore.
Your loved one is in poor health.

And you have started to despair.

Bargaining

You no longer deny your loved one is ill.
But *maybe* you can stave it off,
if you make a deal.

"I'll be more charitable.
Read the Bible.
Give up smoking.

Just let my beloved be as before
until
our anniversary . . . our daughter's graduation
. . . our son's wedding.

I'll never ask for another favor again."

These bargains, usually kept secret,
are your attempts to
improve the terms
of a contract with destiny, fate, or God.

As a reward for your good behavior,
the sickness will be reversed.

You hope.

Magical agreements have nothing
to do with the sickness
or health
of another person.

Even if you keep your
promises (and most people don't),
you can't change the
course of the illness.

Guilt

You may be searching in your heart
for ways you have failed your loved one,
accusing yourself of negligence.

You may even lay the blame
for the illness
on an indiscretion or act
that occurred *before* the illness.

One man confided his
terrible feelings of recrimination—
attributing his wife's cancer
to his infidelity.

You may unrealistically
assume a power and
control
you simply do not possess.

You are suffering a guilt
that denies what you are—

a fallible, normal human being.

You can't learn to love
unless you are willing to run the risk
of offending and failing.

You cannot love deeply
without occasionally hurting
the person you love.

All of us say and do things
we later regret.

There is always something more
we could have done.

Sometimes we *may* feel responsible
for causing the illness—
through poor diet or because
we pushed too hard—

but in most cases
nothing that you did
could have caused
illness in another.

Plaguing yourself with guilt
will not
make you or
your loved one better.

The fact that you may
blame yourself
demonstrates a concern
and a capacity
to feel for another.

Physical Distress

Anxiety and fear create physical pain.

Your mind can cause
changes in the way
your body works.

Your feelings churn,
your stomach aches.

Food may have little taste
for you.

You eat only
because you think you should—
or you are pushed
to do it.

Or else
you can't stop eating.

You constantly crave
a sugar or carbohydrate "fix"
to ease
an insatiable emotional hunger,
to make your grief
more manageable.

You might also experience
long and torturous nights,
   an inability to sleep,
respiratory upsets,
   constant colds and sore throats.

Perhaps you have some of the symptoms
of your loved one's illness.

You feel worn out and bedraggled.

Your body *is* feeling
the emotional loss.

The pain is not imagined.
It is *real*.

Strain adds to *your* risk
of ill health.

Check with your physician.
Have a physical examination.

If you can share with your doctor
not only your medical problems but
your emotional feelings and fears—
your bodily distress
may begin to diminish.

Tears

"I can't stop crying.
Am I losing control of myself?"

No.
You have every reason to weep.

Tears help to release emotions,
unlocking the tensions inside you.

Each person grieves in
his or her own way.

If you don't cry,
it should not be labeled
as "strength" or "bravery."

If you do cry,
it should not be described
as "weakness" or "cowardice."

Tears are a healthy, normal way
of coping.

They affirm your grief.

Intellectualization

Instead of emotional release,
often there are
words,
theories,
philosophical speculations.

Clinical and technical expressions
can cover up
your own real, intimate responses.

Certainly use information
for self-analysis.

But do not suffer paralysis
through analysis.

Reprieve

After you have begun to realize
the gravity of the illness,
your beloved takes a turn for the better.
You are unprepared.

You may have *already* withdrawn
a part of yourself and
accepted the reality of the sickness.

There are mixed feelings.

Unsettled as you are by confused emotions,
you are coming to terms with the loss of health,
understanding
that there is

no day without night, and

no hope without despair.

As you better *understand* yourself,
your anxiety and anguish,
as you begin to *accept* yourself,
even in your own insecurity,

you are better able to
understand and *accept*
your loved one's illness
and respond to his or her needs.

2
CANDOR
Should I Tell the Truth?

*"I never thought
she could handle it.
But now she knows
the prognosis, she is
so much more at peace . . .
and we can really talk."*

—A HUSBAND

"I can't possibly tell my loved one
how sick he is.
It would destroy him.
He can't possibly handle
this terrible prognosis."

Maybe it is
you,

not your beloved,
who can't handle
and share the truth.

The question is not
whether or not
to tell of the
seriousness of the illness,

but

who shall tell,
how to tell,
what to tell,
and *when*.

There are so many
games people play:
"You're doing so well."
"Let's not talk about it."
"You'll live to be a hundred."

Avoidance, fatalism, changing the subject,
denial, reassurance—
all erect barriers to communication.

Games are usually played
for the healthy people's sake,
not for the benefit of the person who is ill.

Your loved one probably knows
more than you think.

You communicate
so much nonverbally.

You disclose information
by facial expressions,
your mood,
defensiveness, and
avoidance.

Patients may learn of their conditions
from cues by the hospital staff,
ranging in subtlety from
nurses' anxious glances and avoidance to
overhearing a discussion of the case
by doctors outside the doorway.

Patients often sneak a glance
at their progress reports.

Nor are they fooled about
drastic changes in their bodies.

They know that
radical surgery
is not performed for trivial reasons, and
radiation therapy
is not administered for benign diseases.

Their bodies may be impaired
but
their minds are not.

Even children sense fairly accurately
the trend of their illness.

They know they are unwell
when they have less
energy, appetite,
enthusiasm.

Through their drawings and behavior
they let *us* know
that something traumatic
is happening to *them*.

Children who are very sick use symbolic
language
to reveal their inner concerns.

A little girl expressed her anxiety
by drawing a picture of a child
locked in a room.

One boy with cystic fibrosis
painted a small child in a boat
crashing into the rocks,
sinking.

Another youngster drew a picture
of a crib
that looked like a prison.

When people of all ages
do not share their feelings and fears vocally,
their silence may not be denial,
or lack of understanding of their situation,

but the attempt to conceal their awareness
from friends and family who,
they believe, *can't* handle
an emotional confrontation,

and even from doctors and nurses
who might become annoyed and irritable.

The sick person becomes the
protector and caretaker
of the healthy.

What a burden that must be!

Your loved one
probably wants to know the truth.

Most patients wish to know their diagnosis,
whatever it is
so they can actually participate in their treatment,
read about the latest medical advances,
question the doctors
about their treatment and prognosis.

Many physicians prefer
to withhold this information.
And yet most of them reveal that
they would want to be told.

When ailing people
are informed of their condition
they generally suffer
no negative consequences.

When they are *not* told the truth,

they are deprived
of free expression and
shared understanding.

Because of the conspiracy of silence,
they cannot express their fears and anxieties
and be comforted.

They are "managed" like children,
stripped of self-determination and control.

Awareness opens communication
and allows choice;

choice encourages rational thinking;
rational thinking reduces
the fear of the unknown.

The American Hospital Association
Patients' Bill of Rights
includes this:

The patient has the right to obtain
from his physician complete current
information concerning his diagnosis,
treatment, and prognosis in terms the
patient can be reasonably expected to understand
. . . to give informed consent
prior to the start of any procedure
. . . and to refuse treatment
to the extent permitted by law.

Who Should Tell?

Usually the family physician,
but *never* on the telephone
(which occurs all too frequently).

Choose a time
when you can sit down
to talk together
without outside distraction.

After you hear the diagnosis,
share your understanding of the illness,
your reactions, fears, and feelings
about the condition, and
discuss the nature of the treatment.

There are no silly questions
when a loved one is seriously ill.

How to Tell

You hope your doctor will speak
simply,
gently,
balancing candor with kindness.

You or your loved one may hear the words
"stroke" or "heart disease"
and hear nothing else.

Later, when you are alone together,
try to recall and
clarify what you heard.

Be careful not to shut out your loved one
because you are so pained.

Another doctor's appointment may be scheduled
after you both have a chance
to absorb the bitter news.

Especially during difficult moments,
repetition
brings clarification and reinforcement.

What to Tell

The truth.
But truth is relative.

Some people can absorb it
only in small amounts.

Be sensitive to what your loved one
is or is not
asking.

People ordinarily do not face their serious illness
with any more objectivity or serenity
than they have shown
during other life crises.

Nor should they be told in a way
that completely extinguishes hope.

But the hope must
be anchored in
realistic possibilities.

To speak of a cure
when there is no cure
encourages false hope.

But their
pain *may* be reduced.
The life span *may* be extended
even beyond the doctor's expectations.

Frankness does not mean hopelessness.

Hope means different things
for different people
at different times.

Cancer patients hope before
the diagnosis
it won't be true.

But when it is,
they hope
they won't have too much pain.

And finally they may hope only
they'll live to see
a grandchild born.

Each hope is realistic—for the time.
Each hope is tailored
to the new reality.

The greatest hope
is for your loved one to live
as comfortably—as usefully—
as normally—as possible:
to be valued, and
to be loved,
in the setting of
his or her choice.

3

YOUR
LOVED
ONE'S
NEEDS

*"No, my legs don't work
so well anymore, but
I can still think.
Everyone acts as though my
mind is crippled."*

—A PERSON WITH
MULTIPLE SCLEROSIS

Your loved one is *also*
in the throes
of anguish and agony.

It is a very understandable sorrow.

He or she is in poor health.

Your Loved One's Emotional Needs

The emotional requirements
of your loved one
may be harder
to understand and
tend to
than physical needs.

After all,
there are emotional consequences:
of treatments like chemotherapy and
radiation;
of the financial drain of continual care;
and maybe of thinking
"Death is better than this kind of life."

The possibility of losing social acceptance,
a sense of identity, and
a sense of dignity
is a real fear.

What torment it can be.

When an Illness Is Incurable: A Breach of Etiquette

A person with a malady that is inoperable
may be ignored
by hospital personnel.

Priority is often given
to those whom they
might cure.

When doctors and nurses—
even family and friends—
see little hope for the patient's improvement,
they may withdraw from the patient,
treating the diseased organs
but not the person.

The seriously ill can be placed in
a state of isolation,
treated as lepers.

The people who are this sick
are often cast into limbo,
depersonalized and dehumanized.

This only confirms their
deep-seated fears of
helplessness, hopelessness, and
abandonment.

Friends and family may say:
"I won't visit today.
It might be too tiring for my loved one.
Rest is so important."

It's one thing for a person
to *choose* to be alone.

It's quite another
to be *left* alone.

Ailing people, too, crave
companionship,
social acceptance, and
especially
emotional *warmth*.

They may see themselves
as rejected and discarded.

Often they *are!*

But they are afraid to share
their depression.

Family and friends may say
how well they're doing.
If patients respond with
the truth—
"I'm not doing well at all"—

will their loved ones come back?

Loneliness may be more
fearsome
than even pain.

A Sense of Identity

When family and friends retreat,
your loved one may have doubts
about his or her significance
and self-worth.

"I used to be a healthy
 parent,
   brother,
     sister,
       spouse,
         child,
           friend,
             person."

Relationships affirm identity.

"What am I now?
Do my family, friends, the hospital staff
see me only as
a sick patient who may never again be as well?"

"Yes, I'm ill
But I'm not dead yet.
I'm still a living, breathing person
with integrity and self-esteem.
I need to be liked for myself.
I need to live while I'm still alive."

A Sense of Dignity

"That means recognizing my needs
for self-worth,
to live my life the way *I* want,
   as usefully and
   as normally
   as possible."

When there is a serious illness,
family members may mistakenly believe
that their loved one
is no longer lucid and
is unable to discuss family matters,

or
even to make decisions
about his or her own health care.

In your zeal to protect your loved one
from "unnecessary stress"
you may say:
"Don't worry.
Everything is being taken care of."

Your beloved is experiencing
a "premortem" death.

There is no dignity
when a *living* person
is left
for *dead*.

Allow your loved one to do the things
he or she *can* do,
and give encouragement
to do things
he or she *doesn't think* are possible.

Let your actions be based
on your beloved's needs,
not only on your own.

One person
wore a jersey in the hospital that read,

"Be patient,
God isn't finished with me yet."

As people
are able to recognize and resolve
many of their inner conflicts,
they become more at ease
with the idea of the seriousness of the illness.

They are more able
to face the prospect of their sickness
with a sense of
acceptance and peace,

as long as
their physical needs
are also met.

Your Loved One's Physical Needs

Life encompasses mind, spirit, and *body*.

Total care
means not only emotional comfort,
but control and relief of physical distress.

Good medical help is essential.

A Proper Diagnosis

The eminent psychiatrist Dr. Karl Menninger
asked his medical students for the most
significant part of the treatment process.

Some pupils referred to the skills
of the surgeon,
a few to bedside manner,
others to the revolution in drug therapy.

Dr. Menninger rejected all their answers.

His response was "a proper diagnosis."

If a patient is not correctly diagnosed,
he or she cannot be helped.

Many doctors have amazing skills and
knowledge in some areas.
But their wisdom may not extend to
all aspects of medical care.

The physician is an M.D.,
not an M-Deity.

Very often the least-used words
in medicine are:
   "I don't know."
   "Let's find out."
   "I know where we might go to
     get some answers."

Don't be embarrassed
to ask for a consultation
with another doctor.

But *beware* of changing physicians regularly, or
flying around the country to assorted clinics.
This may demonstrate your *own* denial of the
illness,
and could prevent your loved one
from participating in a consistent course of
treatment.

A Caring Physician

The word *diagnosis* derives from the Greek
gignōskein—to know, and *dia*—through and
through.

Choose a physician who will *know*
your loved one
as *through* and *through* as possible.

A health professional who will
STOP,
  LOOK, and
    LISTEN.

A doctor who will

stop
to talk to you and your loved one,
not just walk into the room,
stand over your beloved for a brief moment,
mumble some technical phrases, and then
abruptly retreat;

look
at himself or herself with honesty as a physician,
not hiding behind the mask of professionalism,
admitting feelings of uncertainty, and
not threatened by the limitations
of medicine to cure,

and *listen*
to what you and your loved one
have to say, and
not treat you as irresponsible children.

A secure, caring physician allows
and encourages
participation in meaningful decisions.

Obviously, just as there are
no all-perfect people,
so there can be
no all-perfect physician.

A doctor who meets
the need of one person splendidly
can be ineffectual
with another.

Determine with your family physician
which specialist
would give your loved one
the medical care that is needed
and would understand as well
your beloved's
likes and dislikes,
concerns and fears,
hopes and desires—

who would know the patient as a person.

Control of Pain and Suffering

Pain is not only physical,
it is psychological as well.

Whether pain is bearable
may depend upon the meaning
a person gives to it.

Everyone has a
different
tolerance for pain.

Drug therapy is often administered
to relieve suffering.

New discoveries in pharmacology
help many patients
live with their illness
without torment,
and sometimes even without discomfort.

The patients often know
their *own* need for drugs.

Too often medicines are given
before they are requested,
before they are needed.

Drugs should not be administered
so as to distort reality or
alter the state of consciousness.

Using drugs for the convenience
of the staff
is *drug abuse.*

Speak to your doctor.

Share your observations
of your loved one's response to the medication
and inquire
whether the dosage is appropriate
for your loved one's *present* condition and
whether other drugs
or none at all
may *now* be indicated.

The purpose of the medication
is to make patients' lives
as bearable as possible,
and help them to go on living
as themselves.

Treatment can become overtreatment.

To artificially prolong life
with heroic measures, when
the pain is great, and
death is imminent,

may not be in the best interest
of your loved one.

Sick people, too, demand dignity.

4

YOUR CHILDREN'S NEEDS

*"Why won't they
let me see my
grandpa?"*

—A SEVEN-YEAR-OLD

83•

You are not the only one affected
by sickness in the family.

Children are often forgotten by grieving adults.

Having a loved one who is seriously ill
is potentially destructive to their health.

Sickness leaves an imprint on
the healthiest of personalities.

Be truthful.

Explain to your youngsters,
in words they can understand,
what the problem is,
why you are not as available to them as before,
and why your moods are so changeable.

Silence and secrecy
heighten their sense of being shut out
and isolated
from reality.

If possible,
encourage them to visit, too.
They are part of the family.

You will be surprised at the
cheering effect they will
have on your loved one.

The role of children
can be pivotal
in a sick person's ability
to feel vital and alive.

Prepare them in advance
for what the person will look like—
with bandages or sores or hair and weight loss,
with tubes, a respirator, or
other medical equipment.

Children need not be harmed emotionally
by visiting the seriously ill.

What they see is rarely so bad
as what they fear might be.

They may learn that mental health
is not the denial of tragedy,
but the frank acknowledgment of it.

A visit can prepare them for the future.

5
SETTINGS

*"I have lived almost all my life
in this house
and this is where
I want to be."*

—A TERMINALLY ILL PATIENT

Years ago, most people were nursed at home,
and died there.

Periods of illness
took place in the midst of kin,
with the comfort of familiar surroundings.

Today most people are placed
in institutions.

The French social historian Philippe Ariès
describes the trend as
"a brutal revolution in traditional ideas
and feelings."

Most people
would choose to be at home,
in an environment of continuity and security,
having the greatest possible control
over their lives,

not treated just as ailing patients,
but as human beings.

Many ill people and their families
are unaware
that being at home
can be a real option.

There are resources.
Hospital outpatient departments,
medical and nursing services
can provide help for
your beloved at home.

Relatives and friends can be taught
how to care effectively for the loved one and
how to administer drugs at home.

Homemaker and sitter services
will allow you some respite
from constant care.

You may benefit, too,
if you care for your
loved one.

You are giving a gift of
your time,
your self,
your familiar touch.

Sharing your
burdens, joys, and hours together
may draw you closer
and ease your sense
of helplessness and guilt.

Institutions can distance sick people
when
they may spend their days
in sterile settings,
sharing accommodations with strangers,
managed by institutional personnel
rather than family.

Often they live lonely existences,
neither dignified nor tranquil.

The bureaucratization of serious illness
can have a high psychological cost.

But home care is
not always possible or desirable.

Don't feel guilty
if it isn't feasible for your family.

The sick person
may become confused, disoriented, and
need medical and psychological care
not available
outside of a hospital facility.

When a loved one is ill,
family members may be torn
between responsibility for the sick person
and for
the other members of the household.

The unity of the home is disrupted
when the members
can *no longer* accept the added tension
of a crisis situation
and feelings, formerly controlled,
explode.

Pressures—physical, emotional, and social—
may be unbearable,
particularly if the illness
is a lingering one.

Frustration and fatigue
can deplete the strength
of the most loving and devoted person.

Weigh all the choices.
Take time to decide.
Seek support of professionals, friends, and other
family members, including
the sick person—
if you can.

Hospitals and Nursing Homes

When home care is not feasible,
hospitals and nursing homes
may be appropriate places for your loved one.

Check carefully the reputation,
facilities, and personnel of
any hospital or nursing home
you consider.

Look for

—smaller, specialized wards,
  offering individualized treatment.

—Even in a large facility,
  you can find intimacy and
  warmth.

—Surround your loved one with
  familiar things
  that he or she values.

—Decorate the room with personal items.
  Arrange to bring in favorite foods occasionally.

—See if your beloved
  could conveniently wear his or her own
  nightclothes
  rather than the usual hospital garb.

Throughout the country,
families and friends
are challenging the
once sacred
institutional rules, regulations, and
visiting policies that
isolate them
from their loved one.

Long-established rules
are being revised.

Small children may be allowed to
visit the sick person.

Visiting hours have become more flexible.

Patients and their families
may participate in the planning and
carrying out of care.

As closely as possible, attempt
to provide
the kind of loving care
that you would give
at home.

Don't be surprised if your
requests are denied—and don't
give up.

Be persistent.

Speak to the administrator, if necessary,
to get an adequate reason
for the refusal—or a
reversal of policy.

The Hospice Idea

Since 1967, another setting
has been available for the dying person.

Historically, a hospice
was both hospital and hotel.
Pilgrims could stop there
for rest and sustenance.

Today, the hospice
is a place for respite
but not cure.

In St. Christopher's in England
the wards are noted for
their spaciousness and peaceful atmosphere.
Big windows fill the hospice with light.
There are flowers everywhere.

Visitors come
whenever they like,
stay as long as they want
but never on Monday—
Monday is "relatives' day off."
The hairdresser comes,
and the hospice holds parties and concerts.

In the dining room
patients, visitors, staff and their children
(yes, there is a daycare center at the hospice)
gather for meals.

Patients are allowed to make decisions,
read when they want,
eat in the garden at their leisure,
keep their own clothes,
bring a familiar chair from home.

The hospice staff extends home visiting
with an outpatient team of
cooperative physicians, nurses, clergy, and
social workers.

The patients' final days
are relatively free of pain.
No heroic resuscitations
are undertaken.
There is a skillful tailoring
of medication
to individual needs.

No wonder then
that hundreds of hospices
with varying approaches—
some for children only,
some with home care and some in hospitals—
are springing up all over America.

They can create a warm, accommodating
atmosphere
for family and friends
to say a loving good-bye.

The hospice is an idea
whose time has come.

6
HELPING YOURSELF

If I am not for myself,
who will be for me?

—HILLEL

Caring for a person in poor health
is a demanding responsibility.

You just cannot devote
every minute
of every day
to vigilant watchfulness
over your loved one.

You need time . . .

To Relax Emotionally

In times of stress,
it is important that
you continue to live your life
as normally as possible.

You need interludes of emotional,
physical, and spiritual rest,
some space for

respite,
reprieve, and
re-creation.

Try to find a quiet time for yourself
each day,
even "five-minute vacations."
Wind down and try to relax.

There is healing in solitude.

A little withdrawal from
the constant tension
allows you to return to your beloved
refreshed, renewed, restored—

a little different
from the distraught person you were.

Alcohol and drugs may seem to be
the instant relaxation you need
to ease your fears and anxieties.

Wait.

You are only smothering
your pain artificially.

Drugs have built-in dangers.

They may:
Delay your grief.
Deepen your depression.
Become addictive.

Sedation is no cure
for grief.

Overbusyness can lure
you away
from facing your pain.

There are dangers.
When activities reach a frenzied pitch,
the body gives way to exhaustion.

You need time . . . .

To Relax Physically

More than ever
you should try to stay healthy.

Do not skip meals.
Proper nutrition is vital.

Regular exercise releases pent-up feelings
and keeps your body strong.
Sufficient sleep fights physical fatigue.

You must maintain your health
if you are to take care of
your beloved effectively.

Just as important as it is for you
to be alone,
so you
need time . . .

To Share with Friends

"I have so much on my mind.
Just doing those things that need to be done
consumes my every moment.
I can't think of being with anyone else."

Yes, you are tired and weary.
But you need other people
like never before.

Don't escape into loneliness.

Share with trusted friends
your thoughts and fears.

Choose carefully those friends
who will accept and understand,
who will not fault you
or deny your feelings.

Emotions that are denied expression
grow in isolation.

People need people
and friends need friends
because we *all* need love.

Don't "lock up your hearts"
and fail to heed
the outstretched hand of
a kindred spirit,
willing to share your burdens.

As you relax physically and
emotionally
consider also
a time . . .

To Relax Spiritually

Perhaps more than any other event
the loss of health
raises the most urgent issues
about

good and evil,
reward and punishment,
of why terrible things happen to a loved one.

Your religion may provide you
with a spiritual philosophy
that helps you make some sense of
sickness and health.

Beware.

Religion can be hazardous to your health,
when you believe you haven't prayed hard
enough,
and punishment is linked with illness.

Religion then becomes a tool
for denial of real emotions and
keeps you from releasing feelings of
helplessness, guilt, anger.

A mature, forgiving, open faith
encourages expression,
allows your angry cry to heaven—
   "How could you, God!"

Religion offers no absolute answers,
no guarantee of special treatment,
no extended length of time for your beloved.

For many,
faith *does*

help its believers
to accept the unacceptable,
and to ennoble
ignoble misfortune.

HELPING YOUR LOVED ONE

"He needs me.
I need him.
We need each other."

—WORDS OF PATIENT AND FAMILY

A Time to Visit

Illness is one task that
each person must perform
entirely by himself or herself.

That is not to say
that your loved one
should be *alone.*

Visit frequently,
if your loved one is not at home.

Share news of the family.

Seek your beloved's advice,
so he or she will know that
his or her judgment *still* is valued.

Bring small gifts.

Especially bring yourself.

You may find it painful
visiting an ailing person,
especially someone with an advanced disease.

When a loved one's features
change markedly,
it is hard to believe
you are with the same person.

It is difficult to keep eye contact.
Words don't come easily.

You try to act naturally,
but you feel awkward.

Suddenly, your beloved
seems a stranger.

Think of the person
you knew.
Inside he or she is probably
the same.

"Real isn't how you are made," said the Skin Horse.
"It's a thing that happens to you."
"Does it hurt?" asked the Rabbit.
"Sometimes," said the Skin Horse, for he was always
truthful.
"When you are Real, you don't mind being hurt. It doesn't
often happen to people who break easily, or have sharp
edges, or who have to be carefully kept. Generally, by the
time you are Real, most of your hair has been loved off, and
your eyes drop out, and you get loose in the joints and very
shabby. But these things don't matter at all, because once
you are Real, you can't be ugly, except to people who don't
understand."

—MARGARITE WILLIAMS
THE VELVETEEN RABBIT

A Time to Talk

Not with—
   "Snap out of it.
     Everything will be fine, you'll see.
     Try to get hold of yourself."
Chattering isn't communication.

Neither is denial.

Your loved one doesn't need
platitudes and reassurances
that you both
know are false.

They signal your beloved
not to share, but
to hide
real fear and feelings
from you.

Don't try to make life "normal"
by pretending nothing is wrong.

At the same time
avoid saying
"terminal" or "hopeless."

Such words make the dying person feel
written off
the rolls of the living.

Stress
that you and the doctors
will do all you can
to make your loved one's life as happy and as
comfortable as possible.

Look your loved one in the eye.
Be open and straightforward.

You allow an
honest exchange of feelings
when you say:
    "It must be hard for you, isn't it?
    I'd like to help you, but I
    don't know what to do—
    what would you suggest?"

Don't be afraid of admitting
    your anxiety,
    your indecision, and
    your pain.

Even though no one
can truly understand
another person's feelings,
try to empathize and
identify with your loved one's feelings.

Ask yourself:
  "Knowing my beloved as I do,
   how would I react
   if it were I?"

The person may feel a need
to talk not only about the illness
but about
the happy moments of his or her life.

A loved one needs to know
that his or her life on earth
does have an impact upon others.

Consider:
a tape recording of the life for an oral history
to be *forever* chronicled.

Or an album of pictures
and of keepsakes.

These records of one's life
reduce feelings of
meaninglessness and absurdity.

A Time to Listen

During moments of crisis,
many people are so concerned
about *what* to say,
that they frame answers
without hearing what is said.

More important than your words
is your ability to listen
not only to what is said,
but to how it is said
and what is meant, and

to seize the secret messages of silence.

Listen between the lines—
emotional content, body language,
silences, avoided topics.

Eyes averted,
turned-down head,
posture-shifts,
the tone of voice

may speak louder than words.

Allow full expression of
fears and nightmares.
   "Will there be severe pain?
   Will I suffocate?
   Will I be all hooked up to beeping monitors?"

Tell your loved one:
   "It is normal to express these fears.
   I'm glad you shared your thoughts with me.
   Didn't the doctor assure you that . . ."

Serious illness may be a time
when courage runs quite thin and faith
is but a theological abstraction.

Have the courage to listen to things
that are not always pleasant to hear.

Sometimes, all that is needed
is your being there,

and saying nothing.

Rather than a forced conversation,
the best communication
may be a thoughtful silence, and
a tender touch.

A patient said:
   "The person who helped me the most
   said very little.
   But I knew by his look and his manner
   that he knew what I was experiencing.
   There was an 'I know' meeting of
   two hearts, especially
   when I saw tears glisten in his eyes."

A Time to Cry

Tears are wordless messages,
a vital part of grieving.

Pain can be eased
when people are able
to weep together.

Friends and family
may believe that
crying *in front of*
or *with* a sick person
will be upsetting to the loved one.

Not true.

An ill child said to her parents:
　"Aren't you sad that I'm so sick?
　　Don't you care?
　　How come I've never seen you cry?"

A Time to Touch

Sickness can make a person
feel very lonely and apart.

An ill person needs more than ever
to be close to the living.

The sense of touch
reduces the bleakest of all feelings—
abandonment.

Holding your loved one communicates:
"No matter how serious the illness,
feelings toward me have not changed:
    I am not rejected.
    I am not untouchable."

Don't be afraid to reach out physically:
a warm embrace,
a firm handshake, a pat on the shoulder,
the gentle stroking of the forehead,
a soothing and comforting massage . . .

When words fail,
the touch of reassurance is vital.

Hugging, holding, kissing
may be the best medicine
for your loved one
and for you.

They say:

"I love you."

A Time to Laugh

Sick people especially need
lightness and smiles in their lives.

People who have a good sense of humor
often maintain their sense of humor
in their illness.

Somberness
won't make you or your loved one better.

A sick person quipped:
  "My situation is hopeless
    but not serious."

Humor helped her manage feelings
that were too great to deal with openly.

The threat of her future
was no less menacing,
but it became easier to bear.

Laughing together
is one of the normal ways
that people relate to each other.

One patient said to a chaplain:

"You've become so morbid and gloomy
since you heard my prognosis.
You used to tell me such funny
stories.
I'm the same person that I was
before the diagnosis.
How come you aren't fun anymore?"

8

HELPING
EACH
OTHER

*"Friends keep asking
me why I'm a hospice
volunteer. Frankly I
get more out of it
than I give."*

139•

The fact that one person is seriously ill
doesn't mean
that another person's heart should stop loving.

Would you trade in
your life's experiences with your beloved
because of all
the pain and anguish you are having now?

Your love can now
grow,
knowing the limits of time, or
diminish
because of the pain of illness.

This is your real choice in anticipating grief—
to *grow* or
to *diminish*.

"All persons are mortal.
 I am a person.
 Therefore, I am mortal.
 (But I don't believe it.)"

Now you are *beginning*
to realize that good health may
not always be permanent.

The slogan
"Today is the first day
 of the rest of your life"
 is but a half-truth.

Now you know the other half.

"Today may also be the last day
 you'll ever get."

No one knows about tomorrow.

In short, when you actually
become aware of the fragility of life,
you will see your life differently.

There is a noticeable shift in your priorities,
an intensive soul-searching for new meanings,
and the use of your energy for
what is really important.

You realize that the two *least*
important details
are usually inscribed upon the tombstone—
dates of birth and death.

You will not be remembered
for the *length* of your years, but for
   the *breadth* of your sympathies for others,
   the *depth* of your appreciation for beauty,
   the *height* of your love.

Through this personal transformation,
you experience an opportunity for growth
by *shedding* those attitudes
that prevent you
from living life—
strengthening those qualities
that add depth to your being.

As you work through your loved one's sickness
you become aware
of the treasures
that comprise life.

The big things in life
suddenly become small,
the small things
very large.

You are setting new priorities.
Sometimes the simple things of life
become the most enjoyable.

You may not be afraid of
crippling illness
but of the incompleteness of life.

Yet, even with serious illness,
there may yet be golden days you will never
forget.

Love has no rigid bounds.
Love goes beyond the self,
beyond a precious loved one,
flowing freely,
reaching out,
touching, as it flows.

Love is hard,
but
it makes everything else easier.

In the midst of sickness
your loved one is helping you
to confront life,
finding

comfort in your crisis, and
acceptance in your anguish.

A final thought:

A little boy confused his prayer,
saying:

> "Now I lay me down to sleep,
> I pray the Lord my soul to keep,
> if I should die
> before I . . .
> *live*."

The real tragedy is
to *die*
before you *live*.

One woman said—

"Having to face the fact
that my husband is so ill
makes us value our love
with an intensity and intimacy
that we had never known before.
Each day becomes a gift
to experience together.
No longer do we take our
relationship for *granted*."

As you discover so much
about your beloved—
the hurts, fears, hopes—

so are you learning
so much about yourself.

Each day is another day of life
to be enjoyed together
as fully as you can.

"What we have once enjoyed
we can never lose.
All that we love deeply
becomes a part of us."
　　　　　—HELEN KELLER

To Every Thing There Is a Season

To every thing there is a season, and a time
to every purpose under the heaven;

a time to be born, and a time to die,
a time to plant, and a time to pluck up
that which is planted;

a time to kill, and a time to heal;
a time to break down, and a time to build up;

a time to weep, and a time to laugh;
a time to mourn, and a time to dance;

a time to cast away stones, and a time
to gather stones together; a time to embrace,
and a time to refrain from embracing;

a time to get, and a time to lose;
a time to keep, and a time to cast away;

a time to rend, and a time to sew;
a time to keep silence, and a time to speak;

a time to love, and a time to hate;
a time of war, and a time of peace.

—Ecclesiastes 3:1–8

APPENDIX

APPENDIX

A Decalogue for
Helping the Seriously Ill
for Those Who Care for Them

THOU SHALT NOT

I. Be Afraid to Touch
Touching is one of the most comforting modes of communication. A squeeze of the hand or a warm embrace eloquently testifies to how much you truly care.

II. Hesitate to Smile and Laugh
Not with forced frivolity but with the sheer enjoyment of humorous incidents and stories. Serious illness does not put a ban on laughter.

III. Be Uncomfortable with Silence
Love understands love; it needs no words. Silence can be as supportive as shared conversation.

IV. Offer Untrue Statements
When a patient may be doing poorly, don't say:

"You're doing so well."
"There's nothing seriously wrong."
"You'll soon be as good as new."

Everyone—the sick and healthy—should be treated with dignity and not deceit.

V. Believe You Need to Have All the Answers and Solve All the Problems
Just listen and hear what is said. There are times when there are no complete solutions. Accept your own limited self and commit yourself only to what you are able to do.

THOU SHALT

VI. Accept the Feelings of the Sick Person
Don't pretend that everything is OK. A seriously ill person needs to express his or her emotions. You can encourage that individual by saying: "What are you feeling?" "Tell me what's happening to you." "It must be very hard."
Be sensitive to shifting feelings, whether they be sadness, rage, panic, or frustration.

VII. Share Time Together
Talking, listening to music, watching television, playing cards or games can help fill lonely and frightening hours with shared companionship.

VIII. Offer to Help
"I'm going to the supermarket. Can I pick up something for you?"
"I'll take your kids to the school picnic."
"While the nurse is away this afternoon, I'll come over to the house."
Actions do often speak louder than words.

IX. Locate Other Supports
There may be many people and organizations who can offer invaluable assistance—family, friends, church/synagogue, home health care, self-help groups, medical organizations. These vital people and groups can help to better manage the difficult moments for both patient and significant other.

X. Respect the Privacy and Integrity of the Sick Person
If possible, call before you visit. You might inquire: "Do you feel like company this morning?" Never assume you know what the person's needs may be at any given moment. And always, always keep knowledge of the patient confidential.

Communication between Patient, Family, and Medical Staff

*When speaking with physician
or medical personnel*

—Write down questions in advance. Thoughts should be expressed clearly and kept to a reasonable limit.
—Communicate honestly about the concerns and fears of both patient and family members.
—Give accurate medical information.
—Respect the medical staff's time and expect the same in return.
—Cooperate fully once a decision on treatment has been mutually agreed upon.

*Questions to ask about the medical
problem/pain/symptom(s)*

—Approximately when did the problem/pain/symptom begin?
—Where?
—How long did the pain last?
—Is pain constant or changeable?
—Located in one area or other parts of the body?
—What makes it worse?
—What helps the patient to feel better?

—On a scale of 1 to 10, with 10 being the worst, how would the pain be measured?
—Other questions?

Questions to ask about the diagnosis

—Medical name of illness?
—Possible cause?
—How to prevent the illness from worsening?
—Projected tests, treatments, medications? (See below.)
—Need for another medical opinion?
—Prognosis?
—Other questions?

Questions to ask about possible tests

Patients who are generally aware of the effects of tests and treatment are usually less apprehensive and recover more rapidly.
—Suggested test(s)?
—Purpose?
—How administered?
—Risks?
—Side-effects?
—Can patient have someone accompany him/her during the tests?
—Can patient return home/to work after test?
—Possible medical consequences if patient refuses the test?
—Alternatives to these prescribed tests?
—When will results be known?
—Fees? (Covered by insurance?)
—Other questions?

Questions to ask about possible treatment

Consent should be based on a reasonable understanding of the nature of the treatment and risks involved.
—Suggested treatment?
—Purpose?
—How administered?
—Expected length of treatment?
—Risks?
—Side-effects?
—Another medical opinion?
—Possible medical consequences if patient refuses treatment?
—Alternative treatments?
—How to evaluate success or failure of treatment?
—Fees? (Covered by insurance?)
—Other questions?

Questions to ask about pain control

Effective pain control is giving the patient the right medicine in the right amount in the right way at the right time. Proper pain medication helps to prevent pain from returning while keeping the sick person as alert as possible.
—Name of medicine(s) or drug(s)?
—Purpose?
—Special instructions?
—Frequency?
—Risks?
—Are other physicians involved in treatment aware of the dispensation of these special medications?
—Foods, liquids, activities to be avoided while taking these drugs?

—Side effects?
—How to evaluate success or failure of medicines?
—Can prescription be refilled?
—Expenses? (Covered by medical insurance? Other generic equivalents?)
—Other questions?

Prescription Drug Record

Date	Drug	Dosage	Physician	Results

Questions to ask about the physician

—Training?
—Specialization?
—Reputation?
—Hospital affiliation?
—Flexibility?
—Ability to relate to patient and family?
—Fees? (Covered by medical insurance?)
—Availability for consultation with other medical personnel?
—Other questions?

Vital Information Concerning the Seriously Ill Person

1. Full and legal name: _____

   Previous surname if applicable: _____

2. Legal residence: _____

   Town/city: _____

   Telephone number: _____

3. Date of birth: _____ Place of birth: _____

4. Marital status (circle answer)

   single   married   widowed   divorced

5. Language spoken: _____

6. Social security number: _____

7. Primary physician: _____

   Telephone number: _____

8. Other specialists: _____

   Telephone number: _____

   _____ Telephone number: _____

   _____ Telephone number: _____

9. Hospital or health care facility: _____

_____

10. Medical insurance policies, type, policy, and where
    kept: _____

_____

11. Nurse and/or visiting nursing association: _____

_____

12. Blood type, Rh factor: _____

13. Allergies to medication, food: _____

14. Druggist/pharmacy: _____

    Telephone number: _____

_____

15. Dentist: _____

    Telephone number: _____

16. In case of emergency call: _____

    Telephone number: _____

_____

_____

17. Clergyperson: _____

    Telephone number: _____

18. Self-help group: _____

Telephone number: _____

_____

19. Taxi or transportation: _____

    Telephone number: _____

20. Helpful organizations: _____

    Telephone number: _____

    _____Telephone number: _____

    _____Telephone number: _____

21. Full name of father: _____

    Birthplace and residence if living: _____

22. Full name of mother (including maiden name):

    _____

    Birthplace and residence if living: _____

23. Names of surviving brother(s): _____

    Address: _____

    _____ Address: _____

    _____ Address: _____

24. Names of surviving sister(s): _____

    Address: _____

    _____ Address: _____

    _____ Address: _____

25. Names of surviving son(s): _____

    Address: _____

    _____ Address: _____

    _____ Address: _____

26. Names of surviving daughter(s): _____

    Address: _____

    _____ Address: _____

    _____ Address: _____

27. Names of grandchildren/great-grandchildren:

    _____

    Address: _____

    _____ Address: _____

    _____ Address: _____

    _____ Address: _____

28. Names of close friends: _____

    _____ Address: _____

    _____ Address: _____

    _____ Address: _____

29. If married, full name of spouse (maiden name also):

    _____

    _____

If widowed, full name of spouse and place of death:

_____

_____

If divorced, full name of former spouse: _____

_____

30. Attorney: _____

    Telephone number: _____

31. Accountant/financial advisor(s): _____

    Telephone number(s): _____

32. Executor of estate: _____

    Telephone number: _____

33. Location of will: _____

_____

34. Safety deposit box(es): _____

    Location: _____ Box number(s): _____

    Key number: _____

35. Other important papers and policies and where

    kept: _____

_____

_____

_____

36. If a veteran of United States armed services, service serial number: _____

_____

Veterans Administration "C" number: _____

37. In case of death:

Funeral home: _____

Address: _____

Telephone number: _____

If funeral arrangements are prearranged, location and policy number: _____

_____

Other arrangements: _____

_____

_____

_____

38. Internment plot number: _____

At: _____

Owner of cemetery plot: _____

Relationship to owner: _____

If plot is not purchased, suggest: _____

_____

•168

Other arrangements: _____

_____

39. Local hospice, if needed: _____

    Telephone number: _____

40. Organizational   Offices held:
    affiliations:

    _____   _____

    _____   _____

    _____   _____

41. List any special thoughts or requests: _____

    _____

    _____

    _____

    _____

    _____

    _____

    _____

    _____

    _____

    _____

    _____

Where to Go for Help

Mark Twain said: "It's not what people know that gets them into trouble, but it's what they know that isn't so."

There are many helpful organizations that can help you work through your fears and frustrations. They also serve as a learning resource in providing important knowledge about serious illness and assisting you to better cope with daily health problems. The emphasis in the following list is on information and research as well as mutual encouragement. How much it can help to reach out of your isolation to a meaningful support system!

Alzheimer's Disease

It is estimated that approximately one-half of elderly men and women with severe intellectual impairment are victims of Alzheimer's disease. Before a diagnosis can be validated, other illnesses that may cause memory loss must be excluded. Understandably, the person afflicted with Alzheimer's disease finds it difficult to comprehend the changes taking place in his or her thinking and behavior. There will be questions about the activities the person can engage in with safety and how much encouragement should be given to carry out a familiar activity that has become painfully frustrating. Family members benefit by sharing their experiences with other families who are facing similar problems through many of the support groups established across the country.

Contact:

Alzheimer's
79 East Lake Street
Chicago, Illinois 60607
1-800-621-0379

AIDS

Few diseases in modern times have raised such fears and uncertainties as AIDS. Acquired Immune Deficiency Syndrome (AIDS) may soon be one of the ten leading causes of premature death in the nation. In but a few years AIDS has grown from a clinical oddity to an epidemic.

Not only do people with AIDS face the trauma of terminal illness, they are also subjected to inhumane discrimination and isolation. Many are evicted from their homes, lose their jobs, and are denied access to public accommodation and community services. There are school protests against the attendance of children with AIDS. Even though there is *no* evidence of airborne spread of the virus or of interpersonal spread through casual contact, there is a pathological dread of any contact whatsoever with AIDS patients.

The psychological impact of a diagnosis of AIDS is similar in some respects to that elicited by other fatal diseases. Because of the social stigma, the psychological reactions are compounded. Unlike cancer, which can elicit sympathy, with AIDS there is often shame. One AIDS patient recalls that his father's first response upon hearing his son had AIDS was, "You should be ashamed of yourself." There could be even greater denial than in other terminal illnesses. There are some AIDS patients whose disbelief is so strong that they refuse medical care. Understandably, there are alternating episodes of *anger* and *depression*. Anger surfaces because many AIDS patients are relatively young. Ninety percent of adults with this syndrome are between the ages of twenty and forty-nine. Death is difficult to face at any age but a premature death is especially unfair. There is depression because of the possible loss of the patients' friends and family and of a social network for support during the most difficult periods of their life. Then there are the physical and mental limitations—gradual deterioration of mental faculties over a period of months, and perhaps the inability to accomplish simple tasks.

How to Help

The Need for Closeness and Communication

All people need warmth, especially youngsters. Unfortunately, fear of contagion often denies them the cuddling and close contact so essential for even a very short life. For an elementary school student or a young adolescent, televised lessons and private tutoring do not satisfy their innate social or psychological needs. Seriously ill people must not think they are untouchable.

The Need for Counseling

We could help AIDS patients through their turbulent times by suggesting counseling. There are AIDS crisis centers and other community agencies for AIDS patients and their families and friends. In addition to psychological counseling, there may also be a need for legal and financial counseling.

The Need for Medical Treatment

There have been stunning successes in the sciences of molecular biology and epidemiology. Good medical treatment could help to control some of the clinical symptoms through appropriate medication.

The Need for Education

Fear is generated by ignorance. Only education can halt the growing fear and unwarranted discrimination against adults and children with AIDS or those suspected of being at risk. We could call upon governmental bodies (legislative, executive, and judicial) to prohibit discrimination against AIDS in housing, employment, and health and community services. We should support community education about AIDS, both orally and through written materials, provided and presented by knowledgeable professionals. We must ensure that people with AIDS do not become strangers in their own land.

Contact:

American Red Cross
AIDS Public Education Program
(Contact local chapter for information.)

American Association of Physicians for Human Rights
(M.D. referrals)
P.O. Box 14366
San Francisco, California 94114
(415) 673-3189

Public Health Service
Preventive Health Services Administration
(Statistics on AIDS)
(202) 673-3235

•*174*

National Gay and Lesbian Task Force
1517 U Street, N.W.
Washington, D.C. 20009
(202) 332-6483

Fund for Human Dignity
(Educational material)
(212) 741-5800

National Gay and Lesbian Crisis Line
(Crisis counseling)
1-800-221-7044

National Hemophilia Foundation
Soho Building
110 Greene Street, Room 406
New York, New York 10012
(212) 219-8180

National Lesbian and Gay Health Foundation
P.O. Box 65472
Washington, D.C. 20035
(202) 797-3708

National Association of People with AIDS
(202) 483-3708

Arthritis

There are many different types of arthritis—well over
100. The two most common are osteoarthritis and rheu-
matoid arthritis. Many forms are painful and sometimes
debilitating, and some, such as lupus and schleroderma,
can be fatal. Causes and treatment of one kind of arthritis can be vastly different from another. Your phy-

sician can describe the various forms of treatment and what results can be expected from them.

Contact:

The Arthritis Foundation
1314 Spring Street, N.W.
Atlanta, Georgia 30309

Blood Donation

For blood donations and transportation services, consult your telephone directory under "Red Cross" or your local health department or contact:

The American National Red Cross
17th and D Street, N.W.
Washington, D.C. 20006

Cancer

The American Cancer Society provides services for cancer patients including information and referral, and transportation and nursing services (on a limited basis depending upon the resources of the county unit). Hospital equipment is often loaned to patients who wish to go home but require special facilities.

In addition to these general services, the society sponsors trained visitor programs, "Reach to Recovery," and the "Ostomy Rehabilitation Program."

The Reach to Recovery rehabilitation program is designed to help women who have undergone mastectomy deal with their new physical, psychological, and cosmetic needs.

A similar program is offered for new ostomates. Well-adjusted volunteers who have had their ostomies for a period of time are carefully trained in a course of lectures, films, simulated interviews, and supervised hospital visits.

The International Association of Laryngectomees, sponsored by the American Cancer Society, offers psychological support to new laryngectomees and their families.

Contact:

The American Cancer Society
777 Third Avenue
New York, New York 10017

The Cancer Information Service is another resource agency for a wide variety of questions regarding carcinogens, treatment, diagnosis, and community resources. Services are available in twenty-two states. If not listed in your directory, call 1-800-638-6694.

The Leukemia Society of America is an outreach program for patients diagnosed with leukemia, Hodgkin's disease, and lymphoma, and offers aid to their families.

Contact:

The Leukemia Society of America
211 East 43rd Street
New York, New York 10017

Counseling for School Children

Young people are deeply affected by a serious illness in the family. School often becomes the focus of the children's stress. In many studies, not only did a majority of pupils have difficulty concentrating on their lessons, with an accompanying decline in grade performance, but many also had trouble in relating to peer groups. Others demand a great deal of attention from puzzled teachers who may have never been informed of the illness in the family.

Most communities have a coordinated counseling service for students from kindergarten level through high school. Counseling is the core of a guidance department. Inform the department of the illness in the family and the way in which your youngsters seem to relate to the situation. The counselor may be able to help identify emotional difficulties that can adversely affect both educational development and mental health. Through personal interviews, contact with teachers, and appropriate testing, the guidance department may assist the youngsters toward self-understanding in meeting their special emergency. Referrals to other professional agencies or counselors may be in order.

Cystic Fibrosis

Cystic fibrosis is a disease that produces a thick mucus that clogs the lungs and digestive tract and literally starves and suffocates the body. It is estimated that 10 million people are unknown carriers of the gene that produces the illness when it is expressed. There is no test to identify the gene; the only positive identification is when a child is born with it. There is no cure—so far. Children and young adults with cystic fibrosis undergo daily respiratory therapy sessions to loosen the mucus that clogs their lungs. For some, daily aerosol treatments are also necessary to help their breathing.

The Cystic Fibrosis Foundation offers grants to biomedical research programs and also includes support groups for patients and family together with public education. In all of these areas, the volunteer—family member, relative, or friend—plays a vital role.

Contact:

Cystic Fibrosis Foundation
600 Executive Boulevard
Rockville, Maryland 20852
1-800-FIGHT CF

Financial Counseling

For economic assistance and advice, look in your local telephone directory under "United States Government" for the appropriate federal agencies such as:

Office of Children (funds to help cover child care costs)
Social Security Office
Council on Aging or Elder Affairs Department
Veterans Administration

Emergency funds and facilities may be obtained from your municipal or state department of social services. Consult your telephone directory under "Social Services" and "Welfare Agencies."

Guidance and Family Associations

There is no greater stress than serious illness in the family. The motto "Strength to Families under Stress" has meaning for more than two million people annually. The Family Service Association of America conducts a major program of family counseling for care and personal development, the purpose of which is to enable families to help themselves.

Contact:

Family Service Association of America
44 East 23rd Street
New York, New York 10010

The National Association for Mental Health is a national voluntary citizens' organization working through forty-one state associations to combat mental illness. The Association provides person-to-person help through information services for local resources as well as special treatment and school service programs.

Contact:

National Association for Mental Health
1800 North Kent Street
Arlington, Virginia 22209

Trained social workers have come into their own as counselors for people in crisis. Many work within the context of child guidance clinics and comprehensive mental health centers.

Contact:

National Association of Social Workers
1425 H Street, N.W.
Washington, D.C. 20005

The National Council on Family Relations was founded in 1938 as an interprofessional forum through which members of many disciplines work and plan together for the strengthening of family life.

Contact:

National Council on Family Relations
1219 University Avenue, S.E.
Minneapolis, Minnesota 55414

The Information and Referral Service helps stressed parents and children find an appropriate agency. This may be a family service organization, a children's camp, a Big Brothers or Big Sisters organization, a mental health facility, a guidance clinic, or a social service.

Contact:

United Way of America
801 North Fairfax Street
Alexandria, Virginia 22314

Heart Problems

The American Heart Association provides information about heart disease as well as specialized services for homemaking and home nursing services and facilities for heart patients.

Contact:

The American Heart Association
44 East 23rd Street
New York, New York 10010

Hemodialysis and Transplantation

The National Association of Patients on Hemodialysis and Transplantation is a patient-oriented organization dedicated to promoting the interests and welfare of the kidney patient. The organization has over 12,000 members and thirty-three chapters across the country. Their services include sponsoring mutual support groups; acting as patient advocates; providing limited financial assistance; supporting a children's camp; and distributing public education materials.

Contact:

National Association of Patients on Hemodialysis and
  Transplantation
150 Nassau Street
New York, New York 10038
(212) 619-2727

End State Renal Disease Networks (ESRD). The United States is divided into thirty-two geographical regions, each of which has an ESRD Network. These networks coordinate and review dialysis and transplant facilities to ensure that patients are receiving the best care available. Networks have three primary purposes: (1) to oversee effective and efficient administration of benefits for ESRD patients; (2) to coordinate planning and quality assurance activities and exchange data with relevant local, state, and federal agencies; and (3) to encourage use of treatment settings most compatible with the successful rehabilitation of patients.

Homemaker Service

For food shopping, personal errands, light housekeeping, and assistance in hygienic duties, such as giving baths, changing dressings, and helping with prescribed exercises, consult your local telephone directory under

"Homemaker" or "Home Service Aide," or contact your local social service department.

Hospice

"The purpose of hospice is to provide support and care for persons in the last phases of an incurable disease so that they can live as fully and comfortably as possible. Hospice affirms life and regards dying as a normal process. Hospice neither hastens nor postpones death. Hospice believes that through personalized services and a caring community, patients and families can attain the necessary preparation for a death that is satisfactory to them" (from NHO *Standards of a Hospice Program of Care,* November 1981).

Dame Cicely Saunders started the hospice movement in 1967, when she opened St. Christopher's Hospice in London. The first hospice in the United States was started in 1974 in New Haven, Connecticut. In 1979, there were an estimated 210 programs in the United States. A comprehensive national survey by the National Hospice Organization recently identified more than 1,300 hospice programs.

Hospice refers to a coordinated interdisciplinary program of palliative and supportive services for terminally ill persons and their families. Differences occur in structure and/or stage of development. Hospice programs range from interest groups to organizations that combine complete palliative and supportive services. Most programs provide home care services and can arrange for inpatient care when needed or desired.

Because a person is a composite of physical, psychological, social, and spiritual components, hospice care is often provided by a team in which these various disciplines are represented—most frequently, medicine, nursing, social work, and clergy. In addition, specially trained volunteers often play an important role on the team.

Contact:

National Hospice Organization
Suite 402
1901 North Fort Meyer Drive
Arlington, Virginia 22209
(703) 243-5900

also

HOSPICE, Inc.
765 Prospect Street
New Haven, Connecticut 06511

Kidney Problems

The National Kidney Foundation is a voluntary health agency whose goal is to eradicate kidney disease and promote health services. Some of their projects include funding research; distributing educational materials; organizing seminars; sponsoring chapter newsletters; providing financial assistance on a limited basis; promoting professional education; and acting as a referral source.

Contact:

National Kidney Foundation
2 Park Avenue
New York, New York 10016
(212) 889-2210

The American Kidney Fund serves as a financial resource for kidney dialysis and transplant patients in need of assistance. Attention is directed toward in-center emergency funds, transportation pools, and medication programs. In addition they help support programs, community services, public and professional education, kidney donor development and research.

Contact:

American Kidney Fund
7315 Wisconsin Avenue
Suite 203E
Bethesda, Maryland 20814
1-800-638-8299

Lung Disease

The American Lung Association—the Christmas seal people—is the oldest nationwide volunteer health agency in the United States. Originally founded in 1904 to combat tuberculosis, today the Association, with its 139 affiliated associations throughout the country, is devoted to the control and prevention of all lung diseases, such as emphysema, chronic bronchitis, and asthma, and some of their related causes, including smoking, air pollution, and occupational lung hazards.

Contact:

American Lung **Association**
1740 Broadway
New York, New York 10019
1-800-222-LUNG

Multiple Sclerosis

The National Multiple Sclerosis Society is a voluntary health agency whose purpose is to (1) provide educational, mental health, social, and advocacy programs that address the needs of people with multiple sclerosis and their families, and (2) to promote research into the cause, cure, and prevention of the disease. The local chapters provide a variety of services designed to help those with multiple sclerosis live as independently as possible within the limits of their disabilities while maximizing their capabilities.

Contact:

National Multiple Sclerosis Society
205 East 42nd Street
New York, New York 10017

Muscular Dystrophy

Muscular dystrophy is the name applied to a group of diseases that are for the most part genetically determined and that cause gradual wasting of muscle with accompanying weakness and deformity. Since its founding in 1950, the Muscular Dystrophy Association has provided comprehensive medical services to tens of thousands of people in more than 200 clinics across the nation. Their research program represents an effort to advance knowledge of this disease and to find cures and treatment. In addition, a professional educational program helps to increase knowledge and awareness of the neuro-muscular problem among physicians, nurses and therapists, and the general public.

Contact:

Muscular Dystrophy Association
810 Seventh Avenue
New York, New York 10019

Medical Second Opinions

Like all important issues in life, there may not always be agreement on medical procedures. One physician may recommend surgery; another may suggest delaying the operation; while yet another may offer a totally different kind of treatment. What is essential to remember is that it is up to you, the patient and family, to increase the chances of making the best medical decision. When a doctor suggests nonemergency surgery, consider obtaining another opinion. Getting another opinion is standard medical practice.

The United States Department of Health, Education, and Welfare recommends that if your physician suggests nonemergency surgery, ask him/her to give you the name of another doctor. If you would rather pursue the matter independently, you can contact your local medical society or medical schools for the names of the physicians who specialize in the particular field of illness.

If you are covered by Medicare you might call your local Social Security office, or if you are eligible for Medicaid, the local welfare office. For further information, call the government's toll-free number:

Surgery
HEW
1-800-638-6833

Nursing Homes

For information regarding nursing homes contact:

American Health Care Association
1025 Connecticut Avenue, N.W.
Washington, D.C. 20036
(Represents commercial nursing homes.)

also
American Association for Homes for the Aging
529 14th Street, N.W.
Washington, D.C. 20004
(Represents nonprofit homes for the aging.)

For vital nursing needs, consult the telephone directory under "Visiting Nurse" and "Nursing Association" or call your local health department or contact:

National League for Nursing
10 Columbus Drive
New York, New York 10019

Organ Donors

Organ transplants are medical miracles—truly gifts of life. Many thousands are waiting for life-saving or life-enhancing transplants, and organs and tissues are needed for medical research as well. These needs *must* be met.

The Living Bank exists to meet this vital challenge. It is the nation's largest multiple-organ donor registry and referral service. A nonprofit, nonmedical service organization, its goals are to find willing donors, coordinate the utilization of acceptable organs with medical facilities at the time of death, and explain organ donation. The efforts are aimed at extending and enhancing lives. It is not a medical organization or storage facility.

The Living Bank provides donor forms and cards which are legal documents in all fifty states under the Uniform Anatomical Gift Act. Donor forms are filed and information is kept on computer for reference at the time of death. The Living Bank has a twenty-four-hour referral service.

Time is important in organ transplantation. The Living Bank should be called as soon as possible if death is imminent or has occurred. Quick notification of the Living Bank increases the chances of a successful transplant.

Contact:

The Living Bank
P.O. Box 6725
Houston, Texas 77265
1-800-528-2971
also
National Kidney Foundation
2 Park Avenue
New York, New York 10016

Pain Control

The National Committee on the Treatment of Intractable Pain promotes education and research on more effective management and relief of unbearable pain.

Contact:

The National Committee on the Treatment of
  Intractable Pain
P.O. Box 34571
Washington, D.C. 20034

Physicians

The family doctor understands the family through years of personal medical service. The insights and helpful

189•

suggestions offered by the family physician are as important as the possible medicines prescribed.

Contact:

American Academy of Family Physicians
1740 West 92nd Street
Kansas City, Missouri 64114

or

The American Medical Association
535 North Dearborn Street
Chicago, Illinois 60610

Psychological and Psychiatric Services

There are three major national psychological and psychiatric associations with accredited professionals and services.

Contact:

Psychological:
American Psychological Association
1200 17th Street, N.W.
Washington, D.C. 20036

Psychiatric:
American Psychiatric Association
1700 18th Street, N.W.
Washington, D.C. 20009

American Psychoanalytic Association
1 East 57th Street
New York, New York 10022

Religious Resources

The concerned religious community offers a society bound together by ties of sympathy, love, and mutual concern. Fellowships of church, synagogue, and religious organizations are networks of meaningful relationships that could mean the difference between coping with or collapsing under the pressure of serious illness.

You might call your clergyperson, your church or synagogue, or contact:

American Association of Pastoral Counselors
3 West 29th Street
New York, New York 10001

Rehabilitation

For the patient's physical therapy and rehabilitation, consult your telephone directory under "Rehabilitation Services" or contact:

American Physical Therapy Association
1740 Broadway
New York, New York 10019

also

Association of Rehabilitation Facilities
5530 Wisconsin Avenue, N.W.
Washington, D.C. 20015

The Right to Die and the Living Will

The Council of Concern for the Dying has created a document called "A Living Will," which reads in part:

"If the time comes when I can no longer take part in decisions for my own future . . . if the situation should arise in which there is no reasonable expectation of my recovery from physical or mental disability, I request that I be allowed to die and not be kept alive by artificial means or heroic measures." The purpose of the Living Will is to relieve the physicians' specific responsibility as a preserver of life when the patient's sickness becomes so intolerable that death is looked upon as a healing and merciful act.

Passive euthanasia—the withholding of extraordinary treatment—is practiced in more than thirty-five states.

Contact:

Euthanasia Society
250 West 57th Street
New York, New York 10019

Self-Help Groups

There are a variety of self-help groups and organizations devoted to understanding the emotional well-being of patients and families who are dealing with serious illness. Those who have experienced the sickness of a loved one have developed tremendous gifts of insight and understand the value of sharing. Chamfort said it best: "God comforts us so that we may become better comforters."

Call your local hospital, your mental health association, or the particular organization in your community that specializes in the particular illness, such as the Cancer Society, Heart Association, Kidney Foundation, etc. Other support groups include the following.

Cancer Patients and Families

Share and Care. Representatives of nursing, social services, and chaplaincy staffs foster close relationships among cancer patients and family members who become involved with each other's problems during weekly meetings. The group is encouraged to visit its members who are hospitalized or homebound because of their illnesses. Spouses often continue to come to the meetings after a patient dies. Through continued contact with the group, survivors share their grief and help others who may be facing similar problems.

Contact:

Cancer Education Coordinator
North Memorial Medical Center
3220 Lowry Avenue North
Minneapolis, Minnesota 55422

Children with Cancer

Candlelighters is an international organization of parents whose children have had cancer. Formed in 1970, there are hundreds of groups located in both the United States and Canada, as well as in England, France, and Australia. A statement from a Candlelighters publication summarizes the organization's focus: "Candlelighters parents share the shock of diagnosis, the questions about treatment, the anxiety of waiting, the despair of relapse, the grief of death, the despondency of loss, the hope of remission, the joy of cure." In addition to its monthly meetings and other planned activities, the chapter participates in national programs to promote concern and awareness of the problem of childhood cancer and research into its cause and cure.

Contact:

Candlelighters
123 C Street, S.W.
Washington, D.C. 20003

Life-threatening Diseases

Make Today Count is an international organization for persons with life-threatening illnesses, their families, and other interested persons. In the words of the organization's founder, the late Orville Kelly, "I do not look upon each day as another day closer to death, but as another day of life, to be appreciated and enjoyed." The original group of eighteen members was formed in 1974 in Burlington, Iowa. Make Today Count now has hundreds of chapters in the United States, West Germany, Canada, and Australia.

Contact:

Make Today Count
P.O. Box 303
Burlington, Iowa 52601

Transportation

For the patient who may need personal assistance to visit the physician or clinic when transportation is unavailable or inaccessible, contact your local social service department.